USDA

United States
Department of
Agriculture

Forest Service

Pacific Northwest
Research Station

General Technical Report
PNW-GTR-851

July 2011

Nontimber Forest Products in the United States: Montreal Process Indicators as Measures of Current Conditions and Sustainability

Susan J. Alexander, Sonja N. Oswalt, and Marla R. Emery

Authors

Susan J. Alexander is the regional economist, U.S. Forest Service Alaska Region, PO Box 21628, Juneau, AK 99802, phone (907) 586-8809, fax (907) 586-7852. **Sonja N. Oswalt** is a forest resource analyst, Southern Research Station, Forest Inventory and Analysis, 4700 Old Kingston Pike, Knoxville, TN 37919. **Marla R. Emery** is a research geographer, Northern Research Station, 705 Spear Street, So., Burlington, VT 05403-6102.

Cover photograph by Susan J. Alexander.

Abstract

Alexander, Susan J.; Oswalt, Sonja N.; Emery, Marla R. 2011. Nontimber forest products in the United States: Montreal Process indicators as measures of current conditions and sustainability. Gen. Tech. Rep. PNW-GTR-851. Portland, OR: U.S. Department of Agriculture, Forest Service, Pacific Northwest Research Station. 36 p.

The United States, in partnership with 11 other countries, participates in the Montreal Process. Each country assesses national progress toward the sustainable management of forest resources by using a set of criteria and indicators agreed on by all member countries. Several indicators focus on nontimber forest products (NTFPs). In the United States, permit and contract data from the U.S. Forest Service and the Bureau of Land Management, in addition to several other data sources, were used as a benchmark to assess harvest, value, employment, exports and imports, per capita consumption, and subsistence uses for many NTFPs. The retail value of commercial harvests of NTFPs from U.S. forest lands is estimated at $1.4 billion annually. Nontimber forest products in the United States are important to many people throughout the country for personal, cultural, and commercial uses, providing food security, beauty, connection to culture and tradition, and income.

Keywords: Nontimber forest products, sustainable forest management, subsistence.

Contents

1   **Introduction**

8   **Annual Harvest of Nontimber Forest Products in the United States**

8   Arts, Crafts, and Florals

10 Nursery and Landscape Uses

11 Edible Fruits, Nuts, Berries, and Sap

15 Grass, Hay, Alfalfa, and Other Forage

16 Herbal and Medicinal Plants

19 Christmas Trees

19 Hunting and Trapping

20 **Value of Nontimber Forest Products Produced or Collected**

23 **Exports and Imports of Nontimber Forest Products**

26 **Total and Per Capita Consumption of Nontimber and Nonwood Forest Products**

28 **Area and Percentage of Forests Used for Subsistence Uses**

31 **Conclusions**

32 **Acknowledgments**

32 **Metric Equivalents**

33 **Literature Cited**

Introduction

Almost all ideas about sustainability put forward in the past two decades are consistent with the definition of sustainable development stated by the 1987 Brundtland Commission Report (WCED 1987) as "…development that meets the needs of the present without compromising the ability of future generations to meet their own needs."

The United States and 177 other nations that gathered at the Rio Earth Summit in 1992 agreed to take steps to advance sustainable development. Building on the forest principles adopted at the 1992 Earth Summit, different groups of countries joined together to reach consensus on ways to assess national progress toward the sustainable management of forest resources. Globally, nine international criteria and indicator processes involving 150 countries are underway (USDA FS 2004). The United States—in partnership with Canada, Japan, New Zealand, Australia, Republic of Korea, Chile, Mexico, China, the Russian Federation, Uruguay, and Argentina—participates in the Montreal Process. These 12 countries contain more than 90 percent of the world's temperate and boreal forests and 60 percent of all forests (USDA FS 2004). Each country assesses its own forests by using a set of criteria and indicators agreed on by all member countries. After each periodic review and report, the member countries reconvene to assess the success of the indicators, revising them as necessary.

Several indicators in the Montreal Process address issues and measurements of nonwood forest products (NWFPs). Indicators in the Montreal Process that focus on measurements of various aspects and characteristics of NWFPs can be found in two general areas, or criteria. One criterion that includes NWFPs focuses on productive capacity of forest ecosystems. The NWFP indicator in this criterion seeks to measure annual harvest of NWFPs nationwide. The other criterion that includes NWFPs examines the maintenance and enhancement of long-term multiple socioeconomic benefits to meet the needs of societies. Several of the indicators in this criterion focus on value, consumption, international trade, employment, wages, and subsistence uses of NWFPs. Nonwood forest products include medicinal plants, food and forage species, floral and horticultural species, materials used in arts and crafts, and game animals and fur bearers. Fuelwood, posts and poles, and Christmas trees are wood products but are included in the U.S. NWFP indicator analyses because these products are frequently overlooked in conventional forest products analyses. When wood products such as posts and poles are included in an analysis of forest products other than commercial sawtimber and pulpwood, the collection of various products is referred to as nontimber forest products (NTFPs). The remainder of this document will discuss nontimber forest products (NTFPs), which include not only NWFPs such as medicinal plants, food and forage species, and so on, but also wood products including posts and poles, Christmas trees, and fuelwood.

Personal and commercial uses of many nontimber forest resources have been occurring for a very long time. Land managers report that some products, such as wild edible fungi, have seen increases in harvest and attention in the past couple of decades, particularly in the late 1980s and early 1990s (Smith et al. 2010). Data in this report indicate that permit and contract sales from harvest of NTFPs from U.S. Forest Service (USFS) and Bureau of Land Management (BLM) lands from 1998 to 2007 has been fairly constant in all categories. Harvest of medicinal plants in the United States has generated concern, prompting protective measures for many species. Foods from wild-harvested native plants and fungi provide a small share of foods consumed by Americans, but are often culturally significant and are becoming increasingly popular in restaurants and grocery stores. Native wild-harvested plants, fungi, and game animals have important cultural meaning for many people, in addition to providing food security in lean times. Native plant and animal parts used for decoration and art are as variable as their uses, from Christmas greens to antler and reed baskets. In the United States, large game animals are harvested for sport or subsistence. Over the past 20 years, harvests of common big game species have generally paralleled human population trends; the number of hunters and time devoted to hunting has increased. The numbers of small game hunters and migratory bird hunters has declined (Flather et al. 1999).

Duran[1] estimated that 8 out of 10 people collecting NTFPs from Forest Service lands in Oregon and Washington are gathering these products for personal use. Based on the authors' collective experience and knowledge, it is probably true nationwide that most people who gather NTFPs do so for personal and subsistence use. As it is not possible to estimate personal use of NTFP on a broad scale, this analysis focuses on permit and contract data from federal lands and uses those data to estimate national commercial use. These permits and contracts from federal lands are assumed to be for commercial use, but are likely a combination of personal and commercial use. This is particularly true for products such as Christmas trees and firewood, for which there is a minimum charge for permits regardless of whether the use will be personal or commercial.

Very little data were available to assess NTFPs when the 2003 National Report on Sustainable Forests (USDA FS 2004) was written. Since the 2003 report was

Nationwide, most people who gather nontimber forest products do so for personal and subsistence use.

---

[1] Duran, F.D. 2010. Personal communication. Natural resources forest products specialist, U.S. Department of Agriculture, Forest Service, Pacific Northwest Region, 333 SW First Ave., Portland, OR 97208.

published, Public Law 106-113[2] was implemented. This legislation was passed by Congress in the 2000 Interior and Related Agencies Appropriations bill. The act, titled "Pilot Program of Charges and Fees for Harvest of Forest Botanical Products" for the National Forest System, is commonly referred to as "Section 339" of Public Law 106-113. The law defines forest botanical products as "any naturally occurring mushrooms, fungi, flowers, seeds, roots, bark, leaves, and any other vegetation (or portion thereof) that grow on National Forest System lands." Section 339 directs the Secretary of Agriculture to develop and implement a pilot program to charge for forest botanical products through the establishment of appraisal methods and bidding procedures. The act also requires analysis regarding the sustainability of harvest levels and exempts personal, but not commercial, use from fees. The act was amended in 2003 so that fees are not only set by an appraisal process, but also require that a portion of fair market value and costs be recovered.[3] This law has had a considerable impact on the development of appraisal methods and on commercial NTFP harvesting on USFS lands. As a result of this law, all USFS forests selling NTFPs are required to establish fair market values and develop minimum rates for individual products (Smith et al. 2010). Funds collected from the sale of NTFPs on USFS lands can be retained and used to manage NTFP programs on individual national forests. These requirements meant that many USFS districts expanded their NTFP sales programs. Both the BLM and the USFS track product sales in two general classes, "convertible" and "nonconvertible." Convertible means the units of measure are in standard units used to measure wood volume, board feet or cubic feet of solid wood. Nonconvertible means the products either are not or cannot be measured by using wood volume measures. Nonconvertible products include Christmas trees, in addition to forest botanicals such as mushrooms or boughs. The USFS has tracked nonconvertible permit and contract data since 1998 (e.g., USDA FS 2007) and the BLM has tracked nonconvertible data even longer (e.g., USDI BLM 2007).

Permit and contract data from the USFS and BLM can serve as a benchmark to assess harvests and values for many NTFPs. Information about game animals and fur bearer populations and harvest is collected by state and federal agencies, and summaries are available in response to periodic reviews required by the U.S. Forest and Rangeland Renewable Resources Planning Act of 1974 (e.g., Flather et al. 2009). United States international trade data can be used to track general trade trends for

---

[2] U.S. Laws, Statutes, etc.; Public Law 106-113, div. B, Sec. 1000(a) (3) [title III, Sec. 339]. Pilot Program of Charges and Fees for Harvest of Forest Botanical Products. Act of Nov. 29, 1999. Page 113 Stat. 1535, 1501A-119-200; 16 U.S.C. 528.

[3] U.S. Laws, Statutes, etc.; Public Law 108-108, Sec. 335. Act of Nov. 10, 2003. Page 117 Stat. 1312.

some wild-harvested plants and fungi. Some case studies have examined issues surrounding employment and wages in NTFP commercial industries (e.g., Alexander et al. 2002, Love et al. 1998). In 2006, the U.S. Census Bureau's County Business Patterns data reported 2,098 employees with an annual payroll of $71,657,000 in the industry code 1132, forest nurseries and gathering of forest products. The average annual income in this category is $34,155 (U.S. Census Bureau, County Business Patterns, at http://www.census.gov/econ/cbp/. [6/08/2011]).

Access to subsistence resources for particular U.S. populations is guaranteed by three canons of law—federal treaty commitments, the Alaska National Interest Land Conservation Act, and the Hawaii state constitution.

Access to subsistence resources for particular U.S. populations is guaranteed by three canons of law—federal treaty commitments, the Alaska National Interest Land Conservation Act (Public Law 96-487, Dec. 2, 1980), and the Hawaii state constitution. The Alaska Department of Fish and Game's Subsistence Division has collected quantitative data on fish and wildlife species and volumes harvested for subsistence for more than a quarter century. Additional data on subsistence activities in the state are produced by the federal agencies that comprise the Federal Subsistence Board. Outside Alaska, quantitative data are largely unavailable. Treaties between American Indian tribes and the federal government, and related case laws, sometimes address potential subsistence takes for selected species. Qualitative evidence of subsistence activities by diverse U.S. populations are found in the academic and grey literature on regional and ethnic cultures, human health, and rural and community development, as well as in the popular media. Regulations governing uses of public lands, and data on area of private lands subject to trespass law or under exclusive lease for recreational purposes, provide proxies for the subsistence potential of forested lands.

For the purposes of the 2010 National Report on Sustainable Forests, sales of permits and contracts for NTFPs from federal land in the United States were summarized in nine categories: (1) nursery and landscaping uses; (2) arts, crafts, and floral uses; (3) regeneration and silvicultural uses; (4) edible fruits, nuts, berries, and sap; (5) grass, hay, alfalfa, and forage; (6) herbs and medicinals; (7) fuelwood; (8) posts and poles; and (9) Christmas trees.

Table 1 lists the products included in nursery and landscaping uses, for both the USFS and BLM. The category called "softwood and hardwood nonconvertible" is used by some national forests to classify their NTFP sales, but it is very difficult to tell exactly what those products are. As we know they are tree species, the units of measure can be used to make some assumptions about what general products they might be. Tree species products sold by the piece are likely transplants and so were included in nursery uses. Tree species products sold by weight, volume, or by the acre are likely to be boughs or leaves and so were included in the arts and crafts classification.

Table 1—Products included in nursery and landscape uses from U.S. Forest Service (USFS) and Bureau of Land Management (BLM) permit and contract databases

Product	Units	Agency
Aquatic plants	Ton	USFS
Bulbs	Pound	USFS
Cacti	Each/piece	USFS
Other plant	Each/piece	USFS
Softwood and hardwood NC	Each/piece	USFS
Transplants	Each	USFS
Cacti	Each	BLM
Ornamentals	Each	BLM
Transplants	Each	BLM
Yucca	Each	BLM

Note: NC = nonconvertible, meaning not convertible to standard wood volume measurements.

Table 2 lists the products included in arts, crafts, and floral uses. This is a very broad category and could potentially include some wood products, which is why softwood and hardwood nonconvertible data are included. Specialty wood can be used for carving, birdhouses, walking sticks, picture frames, and a wide variety of other arts and crafts.

Table 2—Products included in arts, crafts, and floral uses from U.S. Forest Service (USFS) and Bureau of Land Management (BLM) permit and contract databases

Product	Units	Agency
Bark	Pound	USFS
Cones dry	Bushel	USFS
Foliage	Ton	USFS
Limbs and boughs	Ton	USFS
Moss and mistletoe	Pound	USFS
Needles	Cubic feet	USFS
Other plant	Ton	USFS
Other plant	Acre	USFS
Softwood and hardwood NC	Ton	USFS
Softwood and hardwood NC	Cubic feet	USFS
Softwood NC	PAM	USFS
Vines	Pound	USFS
Alder sticks	ccf	BLM
Burls and miscellaneous	Pound	BLM
Foliage	Pound	BLM
Limbs and boughs	Pound	BLM
Moss and mistletoe	Pound	BLM

Note: NC = nonconvertible, meaning not convertible to standard wood volume measurements; PAM = per-acre material; ccf = 100 cubic feet.

Table 3 lists the products included in regeneration and silvicultural uses. Softwood tree species products sold by the bushel or gallon were assumed to be cones or seeds, as the USFS sells tree sap by the tap. Some of these products could be florals, such as leaves or branches, but it is not possible to tell for sure.

Table 3—Products included in regeneration and silvicultural uses from U.S. Forest Service (USFS) and Bureau of Land Management (BLM) permit and contract databases

Product	Units	Agency
Cones green	Bushel	USFS
Nuts and seed	Pound	USFS
Other plant	Bushel	USFS
Softwood NC	Bushel	USFS
Softwood NC	Gallon	USFS
Cones green and seed	Bushel	BLM
Native seed	Pound	BLM

Note: NC = nonconvertible, meaning not convertible to standard wood volume measurements.

Table 4 lists the products included in edible fruits, nuts, berries, and sap. Some of the unit measurements were converted for ease in data analysis. For example, both agencies sell permits and contracts for fruits and berries by the pound and the ton. The Forest Service sells fungi and mushroom permits by both the pound and the ton, although pounds is a more common unit for commercial sales of wild edible fungi. Recently, the Forest Service began selling fungi by the gallon.

Table 4—Products included in edible fruits, nuts, berries, and sap from U.S. Forest Service (USFS) and Bureau of Land Management (BLM) permit and contract databases

Product	Units	Agency
Ferns	Acre	USFS
Fruits and berries	Ton	USFS
Fungi and mushrooms	Ton	USFS
Tree sap	Taps	USFS
Pinyon cones and seed	Bushel	BLM
Fruits and berries	Pound	BLM
Fungi and mushrooms	Pound	BLM
Pinyon nuts	Pound	BLM

Federal rangelands are an important source of forage and probably constitute more supply than is represented by their proportion of the total land base. Table 5 lists the products included in grass, hay, alfalfa, and forage. Table 6 lists products in the herbs and medicinals category. Amounts of herbs and medicinals reported in permit sales from both agencies are also likely underrepresentative of the total volumes removed from federal lands.

Table 5—Products included in grass, hay, alfalfa, and forage from U.S. Forest Service (USFS) and Bureau of Land Management (BLM) permit and contract databases

Product	Units	Agency
Grass, hay, and forage	Ton	USFS
Grass, forage, and alfalfa	Ton	BLM

Table 6—Products included in herbs and medicinals from U.S. Forest Service (USFS) and Bureau of Land Management (BLM) permit and contract databases

Product	Units	Agency
Herbs	Pound	USFS
Roots	Pound	USFS
Wildflowers	Pound	USFS
Herbs and medicinals	Pound	BLM

Federal lands, particularly in the Western United States, constitute an important source of fuelwood, and posts and poles, and probably represent more supply than is depicted by their proportion of the total land base. Table 7 lists the various units by which posts and poles are sold. Posts and poles are used in variety of ways, and some uses are regionally specific. For example, round roof beams (poles) called vigas are used in traditional adobe homes in the Southwest.

Table 7—Posts and poles in U.S. Forest Service (USFS) and Bureau of Land Management (BLM) permit and contract databases

Product	Units	Agency
Posts and poles	mbf	USFS
Posts and poles	ccf	USFS
Posts and poles	Linear foot	USFS
Posts and poles	Each/piece	USFS
Posts and poles	Acre	USFS
Posts and poles	ccf	BLM

Note: mbf = thousand board feet, ccf = 100 cubic feet.

In most cases, the data presented in this report are only for permits and contracts sold by the USFS and BLM. These data do not include personal use harvests on federal, state, or private lands. The data collected by the USFS and BLM regarding permit and contract sales for what they call "nonconvertible products" are part of each agency's national data collection system. Information on the methods used by the American Herbal Products Association for collecting data related to medicinal products, and methods used to collect data for the National Woodland Owner Survey, may be found in the documents listed in "Literature Cited."

Annual Harvest of Nontimber Forest Products in the United States

Many of the numbers reported here list "permitted harvest quantities" and refer to the amount of material that permits issued by the USFS and the BLM allow permit holders to collect. Actual harvest quantities may differ widely from the reported permitted quantities because individuals may collect more or less than the quantities allowed by the permits (Muir et al. 2006). However, the quantities reported here offer the best available assessment of harvests on public lands.

Arts, Crafts, and Florals

Nonwood forest products have been collected for arts, crafts, and floral uses for millennia, and run the gamut from wood pieces collected for carvings and walking sticks, to grasses, reeds, and sedges collected for basket making, to grapevines collected for wreaths, to conks and berries collected for dyes (Pilz et al. 2006). Permitted harvest quantities of arts, crafts, and floral products on public lands totaled over 620,000 (fresh weight) tons in 2007 (table 8). Of all the products in this category (see table 2), foliage, and limbs and boughs, comprise the largest amount of removals by weight in tons, every year (fig. 1). Most of the permitted harvests in this category in 2007 occurred in the Pacific Coast and Rocky Mountain regions. Statewide comparisons of permitted harvests, normalized by the area of USFS and BLM forest land in the state, indicate that the largest number of permitted harvests for arts, crafts, and floral products came from Washington (157 pounds per thousand acres), Oregon (132 pounds per thousand acres), Florida (79 pounds per thousand acres), and North Carolina (73 pounds per thousand acres). Other states permitted harvests of less than 10 pounds per thousand acres.

Western redcedar (*Thuja plicata* Donn ex D. Don), noble fir (*Abies procera* Rehder), Douglas-fir (*Pseudotsuga menziesii* (Mirb.) Franco), grand fir (*Abies grandis* (Douglas ex D. Don) Lindl.), incense cedar (*Calocedrus decurrens* (Torr.) Florin), redwood (*Sequoia* Endl.), bigleaf maple (*Acer macrophyllum* Pursh), bitter cherry (*Prunus emarginata* (Douglas ex Hook.) D. Dietr.), Oregon ash

Permitted harvest quantities of arts, crafts, and floral products on public lands totaled over 620,000 (fresh weight) tons in 2007.

Figure 1—Bags of ponderosa pine (*Pinus ponderosa* C. Lawson var. *ponderosa*) cones gathered in central Oregon for arts, crafts, and floral markets.

(*Fraxinus latifolia* Benth.), red alder (*Alnus rubra* Bong.), and common beargrass (*Xerophyllum tenax* (Pursh) Nutt.) are all notable species on the Pacific Coast that are used for arts and crafts purposes, particularly holiday crafts and decorations. In the Southern United States, ferns, palms, moss, *Galax* spp., and grape vines contribute to the global fresh and dried floral industry (Alexander et al. 2002). A study of mosses and liverworts in the Pacific Northwest and Appalachian regions of the United States suggested that domestic sales of moss ranged between 770 and 37,000 tons (air dried) per year over a 6-year period (Muir 2004). When international sales were added in, moss sales quantities were estimated to average between 960 and 41,000 tons (air dried) per year over a 6-year period (Muir 2004). Arts and crafts produced from nontimber sources include baskets, wreaths, Christmas greens, Native American ceremonial masks, Appalachian dolls, furniture (e.g., cane chairs), birdhouses, bowls, and innumerable other possibilities (Alexander et al. 2002).

Nonwood forest product collection on public land is just a portion of total, nationwide collection. An estimated 727,000 private landowners also collect NWFPs from their own properties for decorative use, according to 2006 surveys, although the volume of their harvests is unknown (Butler 2008).

Table 8—Quantity of nonwood forest products, fuelwood, and posts and poles harvested on U.S. Forest Service and Bureau of Land Management land in 2007 by product category, unit of measure, and region

Product category	Unit	Alaska and Hawaii	North	Pacific Coast	Rocky Mountain	South	All United States
Arts, crafts, and floral	Bushels	0	130	66,522	2,235	1,335	70,222
	Pounds	4,200	5,600	3,199,993	58,368	173,963	3,442,125
	Tons	0	1,307	499,796	119,646	24	620,773
Christmas trees	Each	0	2,054	48,347	100,773	100	151,274
	Lineal foot	0	0	55,553	39,205	0	94,758
Edible fruits, nuts, berries, and sap	Acres	0	0	0	329	0	329
	Bushels	0	0	0	250	0	250
	Pounds	0	200	1,395,205	25,359	193,800	1,614,565
	Syrup taps	0	10,686	0	0	0	10,686
Fuelwood	ccf	0	17,407	1,547	4,185	12,662	35,800
	Cords	199	270	169,899	247,069	254	417,692
Grass, hay, and alfalfa	Pounds	0	1,500	4,264,452	0	0	4,265,952
Forage	Tons	0	429	0	42	10	480
Herbs and medicinals	Pounds	0	0	5,665	95,700	0	101,365
Nursery and landscape	Each	0	2,853	696,050	32,009	35,733	766,645
	Pounds	0	600	25,048	36	5	25,689
	Tons	0	0	0	201	115	316
Posts and poles	ccf	0	2,270	33	2,751	227	5,281
	Each	0	60	383,589	1,291,772	9,198	1,684,618
	Lineal foot	0	0	43,412	282,900	0	326,312
Regeneration and silviculture	Bushels	0	0	2,260	5,367	0	7,627
	ccf	0	0	8	0	0	8
	Each	0	0	21,015	250	0	21,265
	Pounds	0	0	211,430	36,113	0	247,543
	Tons	0	0	110,811	55	7	110,873

Note: ccf = 100 cubic feet.

Permitted harvests of plants for nursery and landscape uses on public land in 2007 equaled about 766,645 individual plants plus 329 tons of other materials.

Nursery and Landscape Uses

Permitted harvests of plants for nursery and landscape uses on public land in 2007 equaled about 766,645 individual plants plus 329 tons of other materials (seeds, etc.; table 9). The largest permitted harvest quantity of individual specimens for nursery and landscape uses came from Washington, followed by Oregon and North Carolina (table 9). The largest permitted harvest quantity of specimens measured in pounds came from Alaska, followed by Arizona (table 9).

Table 9—Quantity of permitted nursery and landscape specimen harvests on U.S. Forest Service and Bureau of Land Management land by state in 2007

State	Number of specimens[a]	Pounds
Arizona	0	230,000
Alaska	2,111	402,680
California	197	6,667
Colorado	4,145	36
Florida	200	0
Georgia	2,770	0
Idaho	7,597	0
Kentucky	0	5
Michigan	40	200
Minnesota	476	0
Mississippi	1,700	0
Montana	7,651	0
North Carolina	22,459	0
New Mexico	7,000	0
Nevada	3	0
Oregon	39,034	1,581
South Dakota	1,825	0
Tennessee	8,604	0
Utah	730	0
Washington	656,819	16,800
Wisconsin	2,337	400
Wyoming	947	0
Total	766,645	658,369

[a] Number of specimens means one bush, one transplant, etc.

Edible Fruits, Nuts, Berries, and Sap

Edible fruits, nuts, berries, and sap (fig. 2) are among the top-ranked NWFP exports from the United States according to the U.S. International Trade Commission (2008). The USFS and BLM keep records of permits and contracts issued for harvests on their respective land and provide some insight into harvest quantities. Approximations based on contract and permit data are estimates only as they represent the volume of permitted harvest rather than actual harvest. In addition, based on the proportion of public to private land in the United States, it is not unreasonable to estimate that harvests on USFS lands probably represent about 20 to 30 percent of total national supply, whereas harvests on BLM land probably represent between 2 to 15 percent of total national supply.

Approximately 1.6 million pounds and an additional 250 bushels of edible fruits, nuts, berries, and sap were permitted for harvest on USFS land in 2007; nearly double the quantity permitted for harvest on federal public land in 1998 (table 8; fig. 3). Permitted harvests of edible plants on public lands were highest in

Figure 2—Alaska wild berry products.

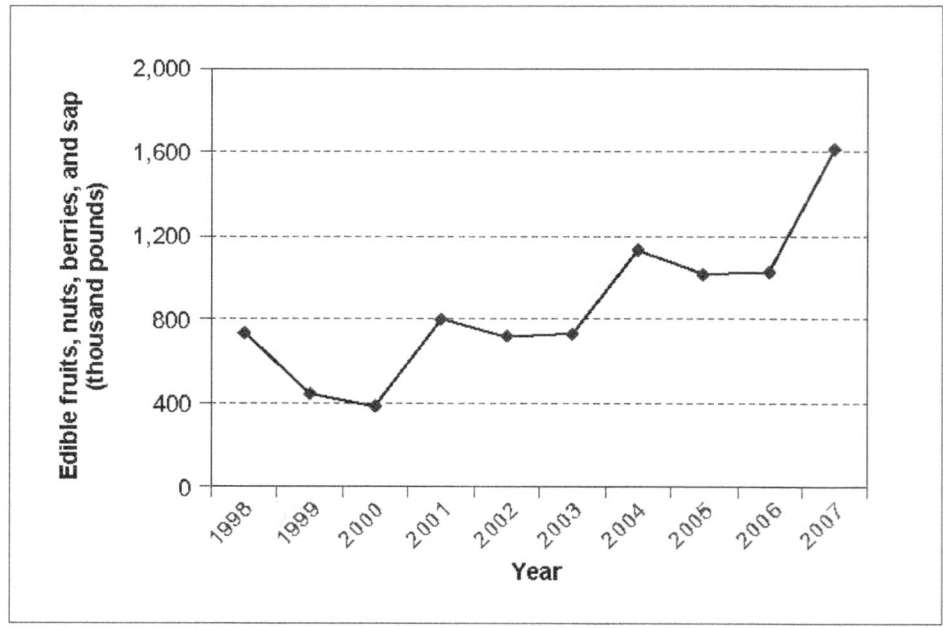

Figure 3—Quantity of edible fruits, nuts, berries, and sap permitted for harvest on U.S. Forest Service and Bureau of Land Management land combined, by year.

the Pacific Coast, at 1.4 million pounds, or about 3 pounds for every 100 acres of public (USFS and BLM) forest land. This increase in permitted harvests may have been more a response to increased focus and permitting requirements from federal land managers rather than an actual doubling of demand or harvest. Although data on the volume of NWFPs harvested on private land is lacking, a 2006 survey of U.S. private forest landowners indicated that, of an estimated 10 million private landowners nationwide (excluding Alaska, Hawaii, western Oklahoma, and west Texas), 10 percent collected edible plants (Butler 2008).

Mushrooms are a well-known edible forest product, particularly in the Pacific Coast States (fig. 4). In fact, 90 percent of the permitted quantity of edible plants recorded on Pacific Coast public land in 2007 were mushrooms and other fungi. Oregon and Washington ranked as the primary states for harvesting of wild mushrooms and fungi on public land in 2007 (table 10). Matsutake (*Tricholoma* spp.), morels (*Morchella* spp.), chanterelles (*Cantharellus* spp.), hedgehogs (*Hydnum repandum*), boletes (*Boletus edulis*), and various truffles rank among the most important mushrooms harvested in the Pacific Northwest (Pilz and Molina 2002).

Oregon and Washington ranked as the primary states for harvesting of wild mushrooms and fungi on public land in 2007.

Table 10—Quantity of permitted mushroom and fungus harvests on U.S. Forest Service and Bureau of Land Management land by state in 2007

State	Pounds
Arizona	25
California	42,196
Colorado	1,083
Idaho	4,875
Montana	18,301
Oregon	712,992
Vermont	200
Washington	494,688
Total	1,274,360

Figure 4—Morel mushrooms (*Morchella* spp.) in central Oregon.

Wild blueberries (*Vaccinium* spp.) are one of the top-ranked U.S. NWFP exports and are primarily harvested and sold in the northeast, specifically in the state of Maine. Wild lowbush blueberries (*Vaccinium angustifolium* Aiton) are not planted varieties but are plants managed in situ in commercial operations through the removal of competing vegetation. Therefore, although wild blueberries are NWFPs, they are also cultivated commodities, making them difficult to classify, and even more difficult to track from the standpoint of long-term forest sustainability. Wild blueberry harvest has fluctuated according to consumer demand and available supply since 1998, but has remained relatively stable through the last decade. The wild blueberry season ended in 2007 with an overall increase in harvest of 23 percent over 1998 levels (fig. 5).

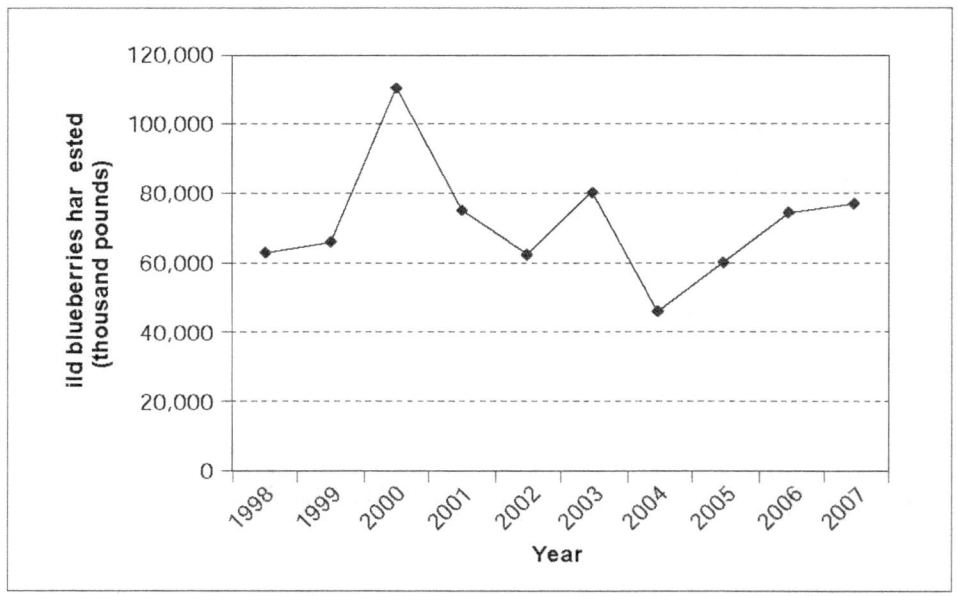

Figure 5—Quantity of wild blueberries harvested in the United States by year. (Source: USDA NASS, noncitrus fruits and nuts summary, various issues.)

Maple syrup represents a large NWFP industry in the North region, primarily the northeastern states from Ohio through Maine. In 2007, 1.3 million gallons of maple syrup from over 7 million taps were produced in the United States (USDA NASS 2007). Only a little more than 10,000 (about one half of one percent) of those taps were permitted taps on public land. Maple production has remained stable in the United States since 1998, and currently only a small proportion of the available resource is being used for syrup production. At the state level, Vermont is the leading producer of maple syrup, followed by Maine and New York. Although Vermont's production has nearly doubled over the last decade, production in Maine and New York has remained fairly stable (fig. 6).

14

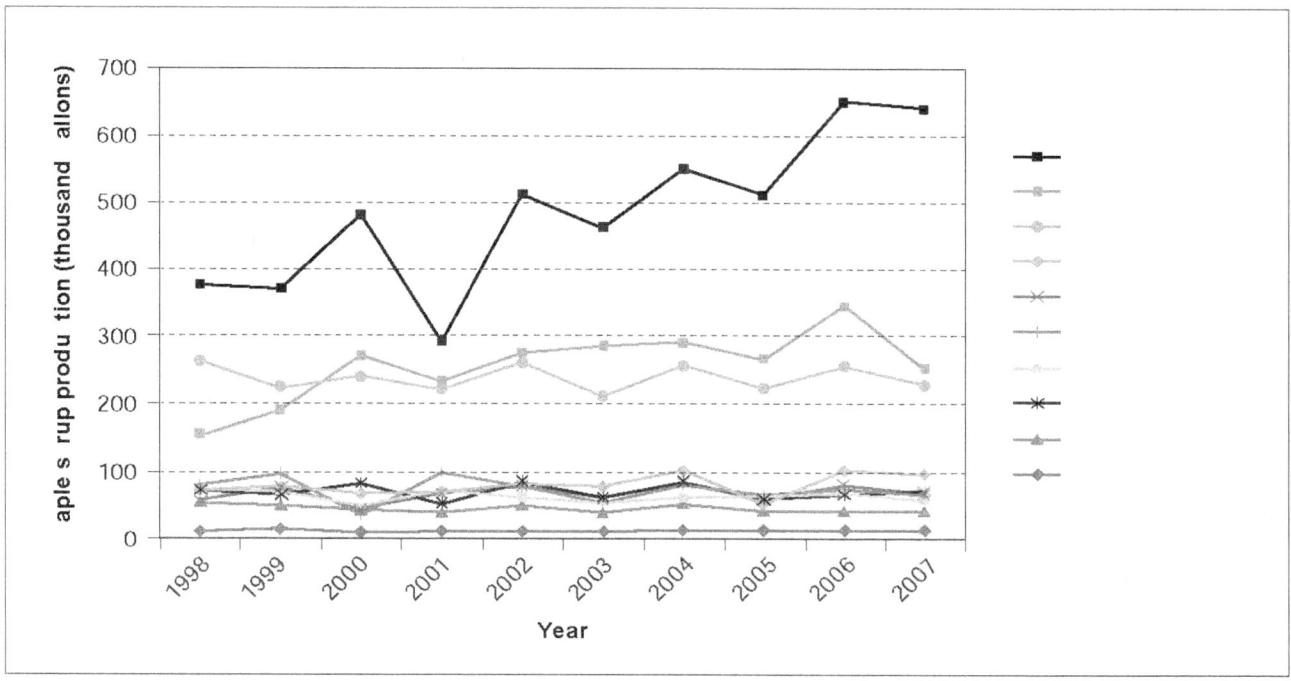

Figure 6—Maple syrup production by state and year. (Source: USDA NASS.)

Grass, Hay, Alfalfa, and Other Forage

Permits purchased on BLM and USFS land for forage plants were included here even though some forage sales may occur outside of forested lands. It is not possible to separate permits issued for forest-dwelling grass species versus range-dwelling grass species. The use of native grasses as forage is a significant aspect of public forest-land management in the Pacific Coast and Rocky Mountain regions (Alexander et al. 2002). Alfalfa, hay, and grass permits were lumped together for this analysis, although some grasses (e.g., beargrass; not actually a grass but often lumped in with grasses in the data) are also used as arts, crafts, and floral products. The data available did not allow for the separation of various grasses in many cases. Permitted harvests of alfalfa, hay, and grass were highest in the Pacific Coast region, at over 2,000 tons. Permitted harvest quantities on public land have remained fairly stable since the late 1990s and early 2000s (fig. 7). The spike in 2004 is due to the sale of beargrass,[4] which is typically used in the arts industry. Much of the alfalfa, hay, and grass grown on private land is considered an agricultural commodity rather than a NWFP and is therefore outside the scope of this report.

---

[4] Duran, F.D. 2009. Personal communication. Natural resources forest products specialist, U.S. Department of Agriculture, Forest Service, Pacific Northwest Region, 333 SW First Ave., Portland, OR 97204.

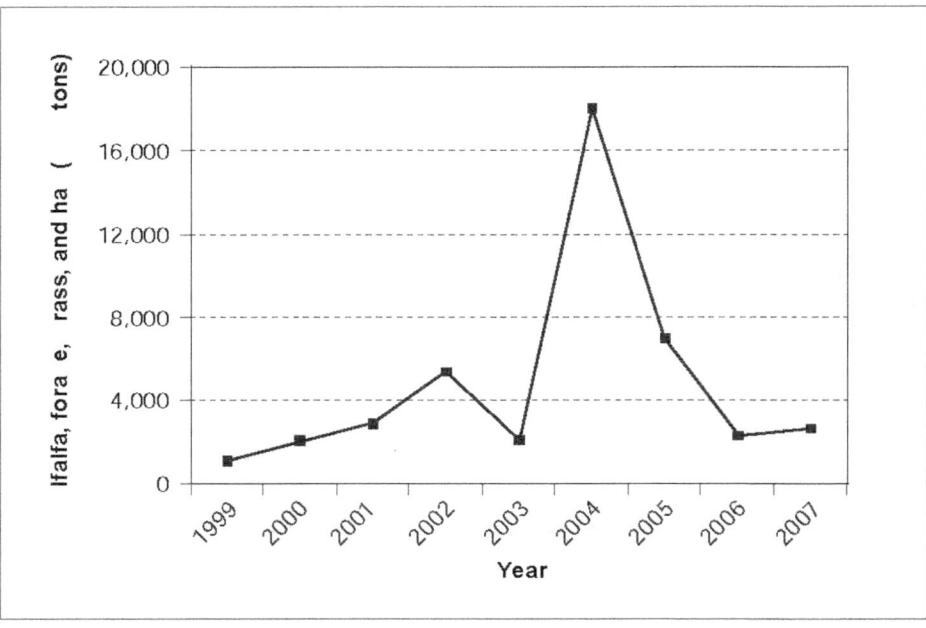

Figure 7—Quantity of alfalfa, forage, grass, and hay permitted for harvest on U.S. Forest Service and Bureau of Land Management land combined, by year.

Herbal and Medicinal Plants

The American Herbal Products Association (AHPA) is currently one of the best sources for information regarding the use of NWFPs for medicinal use in the United States. The AHPA collects information by survey, therefore, respondent participation determines the strength and reliability of their data (American Herbal Products Association 2007). Seventeen of the 22 medicinal plants studied by AHPA from 2004 through 2005 were wild harvested. Harvests of medicinal plants occur throughout the country, although the temperate forests of the Eastern United States supply larger quantities of medicinal plant species. Of the 22 different species recorded by AHPA (2007), 16 occur in the South, 14 occur in the North, 10 occur in the Rocky Mountain region, and 2 occur on the Pacific Coast (table 11). There was not enough data available to state with certainty which specific states within regions harvested particular medicinal species from wild (not wild-cultivated) stock. According to AHPA, saw palmetto (*Serenoa repens* (Bartram) Small) fruit was the most harvested medicinal plant in terms of dry weight (tons). The 2005 reported wild harvest of saw palmetto berries reached 2,893 tons—nearly double the 2004 reported volume and five times the quantity reported in 1999 (540 tons, American Herbal Products Association 2007). The AHPA attributes the increase to fluctuating berry prices and supplies (American Herbal Products Association 2007). The berries harvested from this plant are used in the United States and elsewhere as

Harvests of medicinal plants occur throughout the country, although the temperate forests of the Eastern United States supply larger quantities of medicinal plant species.

16

Table 11—Average annual harvest of plant species wild-harvested for herbal or medicinal purposes by plant part used and region in which the species occurs, 1997 to 2005

Latin name	Common name	Plant part	Annual harvest[a]	Region(s)
Actaea racemosa L.	Black baneberry, black cohosh	Root, rhizome	259,617	South, North
Aletris farinosa L.	White colicroot	Root	1,019	South, North
Aristolochia serpentaria L.	Virginia snakeroot	Root	149	South, North
Arnica spp.	Arnica	Whole plant	21	All[b]
Caulophyllum thalictroides (L.) Michx.	Blue cohosh	Root	6,460	South, North, Rocky Mountain
Chamaelirium luteum (L.) A. Gray	Fairywand, false unicorn	Root	4,529	South, North
Cypripedium spp.	Lady's slipper	Whole plant	58	All[b]
Dioscorea villosa L.	Wild yam	Tuber	42,400	South, North, Rocky Mountain
Echinacea angustifolia DC.	Blacksamson echinacea	Root	50,054	South, Rocky Mountain
Echinacea angustifolia	Blacksamson echinacea	Herb	2,419	South, Rocky Mountain
Echinacea pallid (Nutt.) Nutt.	Pale purple coneflower	Root	9,753	South, North, Rocky Mountain
Echinacea pallida	Pale purple coneflower	Herb	6	South, North, Rocky Mountain
Echinacea purpurea (L.) Moench	Eastern purple coneflower	Root	1,365	South, North, Rocky Mountain
Echinacea purpurea	Eastern purple coneflower	Herb	18,843	South, North, Rocky Mountain
Frangula purshiana (DC.) Cooper	Cascara buckthorn	Bark	197,317	Pacific Coast
Hydrastis canadensis L.	Goldenseal	Root, rhizome	78,699	South, North
Hydrastis canadensis	Goldenseal	Leaf	28,029	South, North
Ligusticum porteri J.M. Coult. & Rose	Porter's licorice-root, osha	Root	3,459	Rocky Mountain
Lomatium dissectum (Nutt.) Mathias & Constance	Fernleaf biscuitroot	Root	502	Pacific Coast, Rocky Mountain
Sanguinaria canadensis L.	Bloodroot	Root	28,798	South, North, Rocky Mountain
Serenoa repens	Saw palmetto	Fruit	2,536,429	South
Trillium erectum L.	Red trillium, bethroot	Whole plant	1,234	South, North
Ulmus rubra	Slippery elm	Bark	189,208	South, North, Rocky Mountain
Usnea spp.	Beard lichen	Whole plant	1,094	All[b]

[a] Average annual wild harvest (pounds dry weight) 1997 to 2005.
[b] Distribution is species-dependent.
Source: American Herbal Products Association (2007).

an herbal supplement for men. Saw palmetto grows in the southern coastal plain of the United States from Texas through Florida.

The top six commodities in terms of harvest volume following saw palmetto include cascara bark (*Frangula purshiana* (DC.) Cooper), slippery elm bark (*Ulmus rubra* Muhl.), black cohosh root (black baneberry; *Actaea racemosa* L.), *Echinacea* spp. herbs and roots, goldenseal leaves and roots (*Hydrastis canadensis* L.), and wild yam tubers (*Dioscorea villosa* L.) (table 11). In 2005, these species accounted for 97 percent of dried, wild-harvested medicinal plants recorded in the AHPA survey (not including American ginseng (*Panax quinquefolius* L.), which was not addressed in the AHPA survey, or saw palmetto).

American ginseng (fig. 8) is one of the most well-known and frequently studied medicinal plants in the United States. According to U.S. Fish and Wildlife Service records collected over the last three decades (1978–2006), approximately 2.7 million pounds of ginseng have been harvested from eastern hardwood forests. Kentucky, West Virginia, Tennessee, Virginia, and Indiana comprise the top five ginseng producing states for the three decades. Kentucky was the largest producer during that period, with a total harvest of 489,000 pounds of dried root (18 percent of total ginseng harvest). In 2006, 25 percent of the total ginseng harvest came from Kentucky forests, and 70 percent of the total came from the combined states of Indiana, Kentucky, North Carolina, Tennessee, and West Virginia.

> **American ginseng is one of the most well-known and frequently studied medicinal plants in the United States.**

Figure 8—A young wild-simulated woods-grown American ginseng (*Panax quinquefolius* L.) plant from a hardwood forest in southern Wisconsin.

Christmas Trees

According to the National Christmas Tree Association (NCTA), 25 to 30 million live trees are sold yearly in the United States (NCTA 2009). The overwhelming majority of Christmas trees sold in lots or stores come from farms where trees are planted, grown, harvested, and replanted just as any other agricultural crop; therefore, it is difficult to separate out trees wild-harvested for use as Christmas trees from trees commercially grown for that purpose. A small proportion of live trees are harvested from public land each year. Permits issued on national forests for Christmas tree harvest have declined steadily since 1998. In the Pacific Northwest, and probably elsewhere, the vast majority of Christmas tree permits sold by the Forest Service are for personal use (see footnote 1). In 2006, slightly more than 50,000 permits and contracts were issued for Christmas tree collection—an increase of 20 percent from 2005, but a decrease of 71 percent since 1998. Christmas tree permitted harvests have declined on BLM land, also. The number of Christmas trees permitted for harvest on BLM land decreased from 27,709 trees in 1998 to 13,866 trees in 2007. Most of the wild-harvested Christmas trees coming from publicly owned land are harvested in the Pacific Coast and Rocky Mountain regions.

Hunting and Trapping

Wildlife-related activities, including hunting and trapping (fig. 9), constitute a billion-dollar industry in the United States. Big game like deer (*Odocoileus* spp.) and elk (*Cervus canadensis* Erxleben) draw the largest number of hunters (and revenues), followed by small game like squirrels (*Sciurillus* spp.) and rabbits (*Sylvilagus* spp.), and migratory waterfowl (USFWS 2006). The most widely pursued big game in the United States include deer, wild turkey (*Meleagris gallopavo* L.), elk, and bear (*Ursus* spp.), whereas the most widely pursued small game include rabbit and hare (*Lepus* spp.), squirrel, pheasant (*Phasianus colchicus* L.), grouse (various spp.), and quail (various spp.) (USDI and USDOC 2006). The majority of hunting (82 percent) occurs on privately owned land (USDI and USDOC 2006), which makes tracking national harvest levels difficult, despite state requirements for hunting permits, and limits on harvest quantities.

The USDA Forest Service recently completed a report on "Population and Harvest Trends of Big Game and Small Game Species" (Flather et al. 2009) as a followup to the 2000 Resources Planning Act assessment (Flather et al. 1999). Results from voluntary-response surveys summarized in Flather et al. (2009) indicate that between 1975 and 2000, wild turkey harvests rose 375 percent. Deer harvests increased by 4.9 million animals in 45 responding states. The opposite was true for small game harvests. Flather et al. (2009) reported that all small game species studied showed declines in harvest quantities. Hare, northern bobwhite (*Colinus*

Figure 9—Big game hunters in northwestern Alaska.

virginianus), and cottontail rabbit harvests experienced the largest declines, with reductions of 86, 75, and 69 percent, respectively (Flather et al. 2009).

Despite the popularity of hunting big game species, the latest studies of big game populations show substantial increases in populations since the mid-1970s (Flather et al. 2009). Specifically, wild turkey populations have increased 730 percent, and deer populations have increased by more than 14 million animals in 31 reporting states since the mid-1970s (Flather et al. 2009). Few states reported on small game populations, making statistical analysis and interpretation of those numbers highly variable and insufficient for trend analysis (Flather et al. 2009).

Value of Nontimber Forest Products Produced or Collected

Value, and by inference harvest, of nontimber forest products in the United States has been relatively steady from 1998 to 2007.

An examination of permit and contract sales of NTFPs from USFS and BLM land from 1998 to 2007 shows that value, and by inference harvest, in all the categories has been relatively steady, with some fluctuations. These fluctuations would be expected with products that fruit better in some years than others, such as fungi or pine nuts. Table 12 illustrates the revenue received by the USFS and the BLM for NTFP sales from 1998 to 2007 (adjusted to 2007 dollars).

Table 12—Receipts for wild-harvested nontimber forest products from U.S. Forest Service and Bureau of Land Management permits and contracts, 1998 to 2007

Product category	1998	1999	2000	2001	2002	2003	2004	2005	2006	2007
					Thousand 2007 U.S. dollars					
Landscaping	786	638	502.2	478	431	382	333	327	262	269
Crafts and floral	1,056	914	738.6	983	1,128	1,095	1,050	816	839	1,334
Regeneration seed and cones	50	21	41.4	41	104	50	30	45	27	31
Edible fruits, nuts, and sap	494	334	364	489	400	428	524	426	334	406
Grass and forage	175	164	197	225	226	228	209	310	242	244
Herbs and medicinals	6	15	17	3	26	27	21	18	14	16
Subtotal	2,567	2,086	1,860	2,220	2,314	2,210	2,178	1,943	1,719	2,301
Fuelwood	3,994	3,639	3,109	3,111	3,105	3,070	3,011	2,878	2,938	3,311
Posts and poles	900	648	678	354	315	399	296	353	284	260
Christmas trees	2,054	1,675	1,753	1,832	1,677	1,704	1,479	1,560	1,275	1,282
Total[a]	9,517	8,049	7,400	7,515	7,413	7,381	6,963	6,734	6,217	7,154

[a] Totals may be off due to rounding.

Although there are detailed rules for how the USFS and BLM determine the amount charged for permits and contracts for commercial harvest of NTFPs, a general rule of thumb that works for estimates of value is that permit and contract values for both agencies represent about 10 percent of first point-of-sales value, or shed value. Shed value is the price received by the harvester when they sell their wild-harvested product to a buyer. For example, wild edible fungi harvesters in the Pacific Northwest usually sell their mushrooms to buyers who set up buying stations in rural areas, or even in the forests where the harvest is taking place. The price the mushroom harvesters receive is the shed value. Using this fairly accurate estimate of what portion of shed value is represented by the permit and contracts sales value is the first step in calculating national values for NTFPs in the United States.

The next step is to figure out how much of the national supply is derived from USFS and BLM lands. In most cases, it was assumed that USFS sales represent 20 percent of supply nationwide, and BLM 2 percent, based on the proportion of forested land nationwide for each agency. These data are only for permits and contracts sold by the USFS and BLM and do not include personal use harvests. The assumptions about proportion of supply each agency represents are intended to account for commercial harvest from all other forest lands in the United States.

By expanding the permit and contract values to shed values (using the 10 percent estimate), and then expanding the sales from federal land into an estimate of supply from all forested lands, you get to an estimate of first point-of-sales value nationwide. The national first point-of-sales value estimates are illustrated in table 13.

Table 13—First point-of-sales value of wild-harvested nontimber resources in the United States, assuming U.S. Forest Service and Bureau of Land Management (BLM) sales receipts are 10 percent of first point-of-sales value, and that Forest Service sales represent approximately 20 to 30 percent and BLM sales represent approximately 2 to 15 percent of total supply

Product category	1998	1999	2000	2001	2002	2003	2004	2005	2006	2007
					Million 2007 U.S. dollars					
Landscaping	35.7	29.0	22.9	21.8	19.6	17.3	15.1	14.9	11.9	12.2
Crafts and floral	48.0	41.6	33.6	44.7	51.3	49.8	48.2	37.1	38.2	60.6
Regeneration seeds and cones	2.3	1.0	1.9	1.9	4.7	2.3	1.3	2.0	1.2	1.4
Edible fruits, nuts, and sap	22.5	15.2	16.5	22.2	18.2	19.4	23.8	19.4	15.2	18.5
Grass and forage	5.9	5.5	6.6	7.5	7.5	7.5	6.9	10.3	8.0	8.1
Herbs and medicinals	0.2	0.6	0.7	0.1	1.1	1.2	1.0	0.9	0.6	0.7
Subtotal	114.6	92.9	82.1	98.1	102.5	97.7	96.5	84.5	75.2	101.6
Fuelwood	159.8	145.6	124.3	124.4	124.2	122.8	120.4	115.2	117.6	132.4
Posts and poles	36.0	25.9	27.1	14.2	12.6	15.9	11.8	14.1	11.4	10.4
Christmas trees	45.7	37.2	39.0	40.7	37.2	37.9	32.8	34.6	28.4	28.4
Total	356.1	301.6	272.6	277.5	276.6	274.3	261.6	248.4	232.4	272.9

These are very rough estimates because they are based on federal permit and contract sales, and the actual value may be quite different. There are several reasons the estimates could be low. One significant reason is that harvest of NTFPs from federal lands does not always occur with a permit or contract. Muir et al. (2006) estimated the quantity and value of moss harvest from forests in two regions in the United States by using USFS permit and contract data, comparing that information to export data, and surveying moss dealers. They found that annual moss values alone could range from US$6 million to $165 million (in nominal values). Moss is included in the crafts and floral category in tables 12 and 13. These estimates by Muir et al. are not first point-of-sales prices, but they do illustrate the difficulty in using USFS and BLM permit and contract data alone, as in table 12, to estimate total values for resources that are often harvested without a permit or contract, or harvested with no need for any documentation, and sold through complex commodity chains that often combine wild-harvested and agriculturally grown commodities.

Table 14 illustrates the value at the wholesale level of wild-harvested nontimber resources in the United States, based on the two steps outlined previously; that USFS and BLM sales receipts are 10 percent of first point-of-sales value, and that USFS sales represent approximately 20 to 30 percent and BLM sales represent approximately 2 to 15 percent of total supply based on proportions of U.S. forested land area. The third step in calculating wholesale values is to assume that first point-of-sales value is 40 percent of wholesale price (from http://www.ers.usda.gov/Data/ [8/20/08]).

Table 14—Estimated wholesale value of wild-harvested nontimber resources in the United States, assuming U.S. Forest Service and Bureau of Land Management (BLM) sales receipts are 10 percent of first point-of-sales value, that U.S. Forest Service sales represent approximately 20 to 30 percent and BLM sales represent approximately 2 to 15 percent of total supply, and that first point-of-sales value is 40 percent of wholesale price

Product category	1998	1999	2000	2001	2002	2003	2004	2005	2006	2007
					Million 2007 U.S. dollars					
Landscaping	89.3	72.6	57.1	54.3	49.0	43.4	37.9	37.2	29.8	30.6
Crafts and floral	120.1	103.8	83.9	111.7	128.2	124.4	120.4	92.7	95.3	151.6
Regeneration seeds and cones	5.7	2.4	4.7	4.7	11.9	5.6	3.4	5.1	3.1	3.5
Edible fruits, nuts, and sap	56.2	38.0	41.4	55.5	45.4	48.6	59.5	48.4	38.0	46.2
Grass and forage	14.6	13.7	16.4	18.7	18.8	19.0	17.5	25.9	20.2	20.4
Herbs and medicinals	0.6	1.7	1.9	0.4	3.0	3.0	2.4	2.0	1.5	1.8
Subtotal	286.5	232.1	205.4	245.4	256.2	244.2	241.2	211.4	188.0	254.0
Fuelwood	399.4	363.9	310.9	311.1	310.5	307.0	301.1	287.8	293.8	331.1
Posts and poles	89.9	64.8	67.8	35.4	31.6	39.9	29.5	35.4	28.5	26.0
Christmas trees	114.2	93.1	97.4	101.7	93.1	94.7	82.1	86.6	70.9	71.2
Total	890.0	753.8	681.5	693.6	691.5	685.6	654.0	621.2	581.2	682.4

Under the assumption that retail values are double wholesale prices (a relatively conservative assumption, based on several sources, including http://en.allexperts.com/q/General-Retail-Business-2223/Price-Markup-Wholesale-Retail.htm [9/30/10] and http://www.agweb.com/ [9/30/10]), all the values in table 14 can be multiplied by two to derive retail values.

In 2003, the estimated retail value for nonwood products harvested in the United States, not including imports, totaled $488 million in adjusted 2007 U.S. dollars. By 2007, the estimated retail value of nonwood products harvested in the United States rose to $508 million. If fuelwood, posts and poles, and Christmas trees are included, the retail value of NTFPs produced in the United States in 2007 was $1,365 million.

The retail value of nontimber forest products produced in the United States in 2007 was $1,365 million.

Exports and Imports of Nontimber Forest Products

International trade is a significant driver of demand for NWFPs harvested in the United States. Many of the most common commercially harvested species are traded primarily to other countries, including wild edible fungi and wild-harvested floral greens. International prices are a primary determinant of domestic prices even for products consumed domestically. Since 1989, the United States has used the Harmonized Tariff Schedule to track the Nation's exports and imports. All internationally traded goods are classified with a six-digit number. Each nation can then add four additional digits to track goods that are of special interest to that country. Export data can be used to help assess domestic harvest and total trade with products for which little other data are available (Alexander et al. 2002). Moss can be used to illustrate issues in assessing NWFP harvest and exports. Muir et al. (2006) addressed questions about moss harvests from the Pacific Northwest and the Appalachian regions of the United States, and also tried to estimate the commercial value of moss harvests. The difference between moss harvests reflected in land management agency permit data and moss information from export data was considerable. Agencies (USFS and BLM) issued permits for moss from 1997 to 2002 that averaged about 220,970 air-dry pounds per year, with average annual permit revenues of about $19,650. An examination of export permit data from 1998 to 2003 showed that a mean of 10.1 to 40.5 million air-dry pounds per year are exported from the United States, with a mean annual value between US$6 million and $165 million (Muir et al. 2006). The value of moss and lichen exports has been steadily falling since 2003 (table 15), whereas imports have been holding steady (in adjusted prices) (table 16). Muir et al. stated that "the wide ranges in the estimates illustrate how little is known about the moss trade. In combination with lack of information about the size of the moss inventory, reaccumulation rates, and species and ecosystem functions potentially affected by harvest, …policy makers and land managers lack critical information on which to base harvest regulations" (p. 212). The commercial moss industry is important economically in both the U.S. Pacific

Table 15—Nonwood forest products in the Harmonized Tariff Schedule exported from the United States, 2003 and 2007

Product description	2003	2007	Primary destinations
	Thousand 2007 U.S. dollars		
Mosses and lichens	4,749	773	Canada, Mexico
Fresh, dried, dyed, bleached, impregnated, or otherwise prepared foliage, branches	96,225	133,031	Europe, Canada
Mushrooms and truffles, fresh, preserved, dried, sliced, etc.	11,109	14,111	Canada, Europe, central America, Asia, Russia
Pecans, fresh or dried, in shell and shelled	83,205	187,346	Mexico, Asia, western Europe
Cranberries and other fruits, fresh, of the genus *Vaccinium* except blueberries	11,905	32,323	United Kingdom, Canada, Cayman Islands
Wild blueberries, fresh, frozen, preserved, dried, canned	41,555	48,198	Canada, western Europe, Asia, Mexico
Vanilla beans	6,531	2,710	Canada, France, Japan
Ginseng roots, cultivated, fresh or dried	16,427	13,640	China, Hong Kong, Canada, Taiwan
Ginseng roots, wild, fresh or dried	27,144	38,274	Hong Kong, China, Singapore
Maple sugar and maple syrup	8,865	8,410	Japan, Canada, Mexico
Pignolia (pine nuts), prepared or preserved NESOI	26	20	India, Costa Rica
Gum, wood or sulfate turpentine oils	4,679	4,886	France, Mexico, Taiwan
Essential oils of cedarwood, clove and nutmeg	7,573	5,405	Mexico, France, worldwide
Pine oil	7,980	11,699	United Kingdom, Mexico, United Arab Emirates

Note: NESOI = not elsewhere specified or indicated.

Table 16—Nonwood forest products in the Harmonized Tariff Schedule imported into the United States, 2003 and 2007

Product description	2003	2007	Primary sources
	Thousand 2007 U.S. dollars		
Mosses and lichens	4,354	4,347	Mexico, Chile
Foliage, branches and grasses for ornamental purposes, fresh, dried, dyed, or otherwise prepared	73,640	96,245	Central and South America, western Europe, Asia, Africa
Truffles, fresh or dried	1,634	7,831	Europe
Mushrooms, fresh or dried	15,252	26,277	Canada, Asia, western Europe
Pecans, fresh or dried, in shell and shelled	98,112	147,267	Mexico
Pignolia (pine nuts), fresh, preserved, or dried, in shell or shelled	33,469	54,010	China, Spain, Turkey
Wild blueberries, fresh, frozen, dried, canned	53,824	109,392	Canada, Chile, China, Europe
Cranberries, fresh or frozen	30,956	49,205	Canada
Fruits of the genus *Vaccinium*, fresh, NESOI	258	332	Western Europe
Vanilla beans	325,333	42,690	Madagascar, Uganda, Indonesia
Ginseng roots, cultivated, fresh or dried, whole, cut, crushed or powdered	13,904	15,473	China, Taiwan, Hong Kong, Canada
Ginseng roots, wild, fresh or dried, whole, cut, crushed or powdered	596	9,781	China, Hong Kong
Maple syrup, blended or not	91,990	141,924	Canada
Maple sugar NESOI	171	740	Canada
Essential oils of cedarwood	215	1,760	Canada, Switzerland, China
Gum, wood or sulfate turpentine oils	4,125	3,857	Canada, China, Brazil
Pine oil	775	2,069	China, Hong Kong

Note: NESOI = not elsewhere specified or indicated.

Northwest and the Appalachian regions, contributing income and jobs. The authors suggested further research is needed on the resource and its response to harvest, harvester knowledge and potential education opportunities, moss cultivation, harvest and trade data collection, and collected moss characteristics. This same lack of knowledge has been noted about other wild-harvested nonwood products traded in commercial markets, such as floral greens and mushrooms. There are several site- and species-specific studies that have been done since 2003 to address these gaps (e.g., Ballard and Huntsinger 2006, Jones and Lynch 2007). The USFS Pacific Northwest Region does not sell lichen permits, and after a decade-long assessment of moss (see Peck 2006, Peck and Muir 2007, Peck and Muir 2008), only one national forest in the region sells moss permits (see footnote 1).

Imports listed in this report focus on nontimber products from species native to North America, even if they have been domesticated elsewhere. Tables 15 and 16 list values for NWFPs exported from and imported to the United States in 2003 and 2007. The list includes nonwood products from native species growing wild in forests, forest openings, and woodlands; products from select native species grown agriculturally; and select products from native species growing in nonforest environments, whether wild or domesticated. Some trade codes are so broad that it is impossible to describe trade in specific species. For example, fresh foliage and branches (HTC 0604.91.0000) covers many species, wild and domesticated, from forests and agricultural lands. Some codes may include products that are grown in agroforestry environments, intentionally sown but allowed to grow in wild-simulated environments, such as wild ginseng (HTC 1211.20.0040). Only a few wild-harvested NWFPs, such as fresh wild blueberries (HTC 0810.40.0024), have exclusive trade codes. The U.S. mushroom trade data since 2002 has split out the most commonly domesticated mushrooms, including the white button mushroom common in grocery stores (*Agaricus* spp.), wood ears (*Auricularia* spp.), and jelly fungus (*Tremella* spp.). Mushroom trade data in tables 15 and 16 do not include these domesticated species, and can be assumed to be highly influenced by wild-harvested fungi such as morels (*Morchella* spp.), chanterelles (*Cantharellus* spp.), American matsutake (*Tricholoma magivelare*), and various truffle species.

> **The top four nontimber forest products that can be identified in trade data exported from the United States in both 2003 and in 2007 were pecans, foliage and branches, wild blueberries, and wild ginseng.**

The top four NWFPs that can be identified in trade data exported from the United States in both 2003 and in 2007 were pecans (*Carya illinoinensis*), foliage and branches, wild blueberries, and wild ginseng (table 15). Export values in all four product categories increased from 2003 to 2007. The top four NWFP imports from other countries into the United States in 2003 were vanilla beans (*Vanilla* spp.), pecans, maple syrup products, and foliage and branches. The top four imports in 2007 were pecans, maple syrup products, wild blueberries, and foliage and braches (table 16). Vanilla beans come primarily from Madagascar, and imports of vanilla beans from that country have dropped precipitously since cyclone Hudda in 2003 devastated Madagascar's vanilla-growing regions. Import values for the other top imports increased between 2003 and 2007.

Total and Per Capita Consumption of Nontimber and Nonwood Forest Products

The purpose of estimating consumption of NWFPs is to illustrate the importance of forests as sources of products other than wood and wood products. Total consumption is estimated as domestic production plus imports, minus exports. Per capita consumption is the ratio of volume consumed and national population.

To calculate the impact of NWFP trade on total consumption, it was assumed the products in table 15 are representative of all NWFP exports, and table 16 represents all NWFP imports. This is an imperfect assumption, as NWFPs may constitute parts of many export and import trade code data, but it is not possible to split NWFPs out of all categories. The United States is a net importer of NWFPs, as can be seen in table 17. The net value of U.S. NWFP trade (imports minus exports) is heavily influenced by vanilla, most of which is imported. The total wholesale values adjusted for trade reported in table 17 are wholesale values from table 14 plus net trade.

Table 17—United States nonwood forest product trade, adjusted wholesale value

Value description	2003	2004	2005	2006	2007
	Million 2007 U.S. dollars				
U.S. imports minus exports	275.2	225.1	75.3	108.3	60.6
Total wholesale value adjusted for trade	519.4	466.2	286.5	296.2	314.6
Total wholesale value adjusted for trade, plus firewood, posts and poles, and Christmas trees	960.8	879.1	696.5	689.5	743.0

Table 18 shows an estimate of per capita consumption of NWFPs and NTFPs in the United States. The estimates of per capita consumption are based on the total wholesale values reported in table 17, divided by population. The values for per capita consumption reported in table 18 should be considered a lower bound estimate as they do not include personal use, undocumented harvest, and certain products that cannot be differentiated in the trade data.

Table 18—United States population and per capita consumption of nonwood and nontimber forest products, adjusted for trade, in wholesale 2007 U.S. dollars

Population and consumption	2003	2004	2005	2006	2007
U.S. population (millions) (http://factfinder.census.gov/)	290.4	293. 2	295. 9	298.8	301.6
Annual U.S. per capita consumption of nonwood forest products	$1.79	$1.59	$0.97	$0.99	$1.04
Annual U.S. per capita consumption of nontimber forest products	$3.31	$3.00	$2.35	$2.31	$2.46

These consumption estimates are quite uncertain because error in any of several assumptions could strongly influence the result. Most of the products and species harvested are from specific regions of the United States. For example, moss harvests take place primarily in the Pacific Northwest and the Appalachian areas, and maple sap comes from the northeastern United States. However, demand and prices are set globally for internationally traded species and products, and U.S. supply generally has little to no influence on price. As domestic local markets develop, regional consumption of locally wild-harvested products, such as wild edible fungi, has become more common. Interest in personal health, sustainability, and connection to land has spurred increased demand for health and food products that have wild-harvested ingredients or some connection to wildness. Although it does fluctuate, international demand for significant cultural or traditional resources such

International trade in nontimber forest products influences sustainable forest practices (or the lack thereof) throughout the world.

as vanilla, matsutake mushrooms, or American ginseng, continues even during economic downturns. Trade in NWFPs has been a small but regionally important part of the U.S. economy for generations. International trade in species native to North America is subject to many different influences including globalization of labor markets, movement of processing to countries with competitive advantages, and changes in taste or style. International trade in NWFPs, in turn, influences sustainable forest practices (or the lack thereof) throughout the world.

Area and Percentage of Forests Used for Subsistence Uses

Throughout the United States, people from diverse ethnic backgrounds make use of subsistence resources for food, medicine, and other purposes (fig. 10). These activities have particular importance for indigenous peoples. Subsistence activities tend to be associated with poverty in the popular imagination. However, many who hunt, fish, trap, and gather to meet their basic needs regard these practices as a form of wealth, which frequently benefits not only the individual but also extended family and a larger community.

Research on subsistence suggests that it should be regarded as a process encompassing preharvest planning, postharvest sharing and any associated ceremonies or celebrations, in addition to the physical acts of hunting, fishing, trapping, and

Figure 10—Picking pawpaw (*Asimina triloba* (L.) Dunal) fruits in northern Ohio.

gathering (Emery and Pierce 2005). Subsistence processes can be central to the preservation of family and cultural traditions. The material resources provided by subsistence activities are valued for their unique qualities (e.g., taste and connections to place and the passage of the season), as well as the independence and autonomy they can confer (Emery and Pierce 2005).

The number of subsistence practitioners in the United States is unknown. Alaska is the only place in the United States where regular and systematic data on subsistence activities are collected. In 2000, the Alaska Department of Fish and Game's Subsistence Division reported that 60 percent of rural households in Alaska harvest game and 83 percent harvest fish (Wolfe 2000). When gift-giving and sharing—principle traits of subsistence systems—are considered, nearly 86 percent of Alaskan households use game and 95 percent use fish. Research estimates total annual subsistence harvests by rural residents at the end of the 20th century at 375 pounds of food per person (Wolfe 2001). That harvest breaks down as follows: roughly 60 percent, by usable weight, is fish, followed by land mammals (20 percent), marine mammals (14 percent), birds (2 percent), shellfish (2 percent), and plants (2 percent). Among communities in south-central and southeastern Alaska, nearly 80 percent of the population participates in the harvest or use of plants and plant materials for subsistence, with annual per capita harvests ranging from scores of pounds to a high of nearly 600 pounds (Schroeder 2002) (fig. 11). Outside Alaska,

Figure 11—Berry picker in a patch of lingonberries (*Vaccinium vitis-idaea* L.) in northwestern Alaska.

research into subsistence is fragmentary but suggests that rich traditions persist in regions including Appalachia (Emery et al. 2003, Hufford 2000), the Deep South (Brown et al. 1998, Forsyth et al. 1998), and the Southwest (Peña 1999, Raish 2000). Research is needed to characterize and quantify subsistence in these areas and in cities throughout the Nation.

Areas and ownerships used for subsistence include both public and private lands. In general, access to subsistence resources on industrial and family forest lands appears to be declining owing to changes in land use that include increased posting against trespass for privacy and liability reasons and growing use of exclusive hunting leases (Butler 2008, Capozzi and Dawson 2001, Morrison et al. 2002). As access to private lands diminishes, some subsistence harvesting may be increasing on public lands. Regulations such as season limits, bag limits, size limits, permit costs, and equipment restrictions apply on all land ownerships. Typically set based on assumptions about recreational uses, these regulations may also pose barriers to the legal pursuit of subsistence activities (Emery and Pierce 2005). Access on public lands may be limited further by management and administrative policies such as permit programs that do not accommodate subsistence needs.

Within these broad contours, there is a great deal of variation in legal access to subsistence resources. In Alaska, the Alaska National Interest Land Conservation Act (Public Law 96-487 [Dec. 2, 1980]) provides for the subsistence use of federal forest resources by all rural Alaskans regardless of race or income, whereas the state of Alaska allows both rural and urban residents access to most state lands for subsistence harvest. The importance of subsistence in Alaska is suggested by ongoing controversies and legal actions surrounding allocation of fish and game resources to commercial, recreational, and subsistence users. A sweeping review of the federal subsistence program in Alaska was initiated by the Department of the Interior in October 2009. As of this writing, results from the review had not been announced.

The Hawaii State Constitution protects the customary and traditional rights of Native Hawaiians, including subsistence use of marine and terrestrial resources and subsistence fishing, hunting, and gathering, which continue to be practiced by Native Hawaiians. However, the issue is controversial in the islands and has resulted in a number of court cases pitting traditional rights against private property rights.

Some Native American tribes explicitly retain treaty rights to hunt, fish, trap, and gather on off-reservation lands in the United States. In addition, it has been argued that federal trust responsibilities and laws including the American Indian Religious Freedom Act and the National Historic Preservation Act extend this requirement for guaranteed access to culturally important natural resources to all federally recognized tribes and their members. The Native American Fish and Wildlife Society and its affiliate organizations were founded to safeguard the legal and ecological bases for practices that American Indians and Alaska Natives consider fundamental to their survival as peoples. In practice, Native American rights to subsistence resources often have been the focus of legal disputes, although several legal tests have upheld treaty rights to subsistence practices.[5]

In the Lower 48 States, the legal basis for access to subsistence resources outside federal Indian law is limited. Nevertheless, evidence suggests that subsistence use of forests occurs in all parts of the country and factors such as high unemployment and increasing food and fuel costs could potentially spur an increase in subsistence use of forests. Whether motivated by economic need, cultural preservation, or a combination of the two, subsistence hunting, fishing, trapping, and gathering persist and are vital to the material and social well-being of diverse peoples in the United States.

Conclusions

The harvest of NTFPs is a significant activity in the United States. The retail value of commercial harvests of NTFPs from U.S. forest lands is estimated at $1.4 billion annually. In the Northwestern United States, significant commercial products include evergreen boughs, floral greens, moss, and wild edible fungi. In the Northeastern United States, evergreen boughs, maple syrup, wild blueberries, and medicinal plants such as wild American ginseng are important to local economies. In the southwest, posts and poles, medicinal plants, and forage are important to local communities. Medicinal plants such as saw palmetto, floral greens such as galax, and pine needles for nursery applications are harvested for commercial use in the southeast. Nontimber forest products, including pecans, foliage, wild blueberries, wild ginseng, and wild edible fungi are exported from the United States to countries all over the world. It is generally believed that both legal and illegal harvest of medicinal plants in the United States has expanded considerably in the past 20 years, prompting protective measures for many species. Permit and contract sales of NTFPs from USFS and BLM lands from 1998 to 2007 indicate that harvests in all categories have been fairly constant in the past 10 years. Native plants and fungi constitute a small percentage of foods consumed by Americans but are often culturally significant. Native wild-harvested plants, fungi, and game

Subsistence hunting, fishing, trapping, and gathering persist and are vital to the material and social well-being of diverse peoples in the United States.

---

[5] Examples include *Sohappy* v. *Smith*, 302 F. Supp. 899 (D. Or. 1969); *United States* v. *Washington*, 384 F. Supp. 312 (W.D. Wash 1974; often referred to as the "Boldt Decision"); *Lac Courte Oreilles Band* v. *Voigt*, 700 F. 2d 341 (7th Cir. 1983); *United States* v. *Washington*, 157 F. 3d 630 (9th Cir. 1998); and *Minnesota* v. *Mille Lacs Band of Chippewa Indians*, 526 U.S. 172 (1999).

are important in traditions and culture and can provide food security in lean times. Nontimber forest products in the United States are important to many people throughout the country for personal, cultural, and commercial uses, providing food security, beauty, connection to culture and tradition, and income.

Acknowledgments

Helen (OJ) Kelly, USFS Washington office Financial Services, supplied a report derived from USFS national permit and contract data each year for several years. Pat Cunningham, a mathematical statistician with the USFS Pacific Northwest Research Station in Corvallis, Oregon, helped tremendously with cleaning and summarizing USFS permit and contract data. Sharon Cordell, timber sale accountant in the USFS Alaska Region, helped with interpreting the USFS data. Dick Watson, a forester in the national Operations Center with the BLM, supplied cleaned data reports from BLM permit and contract sales nationwide. The USFS Pacific Northwest Research Station provided funding to publish this report. We appreciate the thoughtful and helpful comments from reviewers, including Rebecca McLain with the Institute for Culture and Ecology in Portland, Oregon, Frank Duran with the USFS Pacific Northwest Region, in Portland, Oregon, and Michael McGuffin, president of the American Herbal Products Association, Silver Spring, Maryland. Numerous other people have provided advice, comments, and assistance. Any errors in this report are the sole responsibility of the authors.

Metric Equivalents

When you know:	Multiply by:	To get:
Acres	0.405	Hectares
Board feet	0.0024	Cubic meters
Cubic feet	0.0283	Cubic meters
Gallons	3.78	Liters
Pounds	454	Grams
Pounds	0.454	Kilograms
Tons	907	Kilograms
Tons	0.907	Tonnes or megagrams
Pounds per acre	1.12	Kilograms per hectare

Literature Cited

Alexander, S.J.; Weigand, J.; Blatner, K.A. 2002. Nontimber forest product commerce. In: Jones, E.T.; McLain, R.J.; Weigand, J., eds. Nontimber forest products of the United States. Lawrence, KS: University Press of Kansas: 115–150.

American Herbal Products Association. 2007. Tonnage survey of select North American wild-harvested plants, 2004–2005. Silver Spring, MD. 25 p.

Ballard, H.L.; Huntsinger, L. 2006. Salal harvester local ecological knowledge, harvest practices and understory management on the Olympic Peninsula, Washington. Human Ecology. 34: 529–547.

Brown, R.B.; Xu, X.; Toth, J.F. 1998. Lifestyle options and economic strategies: subsistence activities in the Mississippi Delta. Rural Sociology. 63: 599–623.

Butler, B.J. 2008. Family forest owners of the United States, 2006. Gen. Tech. Rep. NRS-GTR-27. Newtown Square, PA: U.S. Department of Agriculture, Forest Service, Northern Research Station. 72 p.

Capozzi, S.; Dawson, C.P. 2001. Recreational leasing of industrial forest lands in New York State. In: Gerard, K., ed. Proceedings of the 2000 Northeastern recreation research symposium. Gen. Tech. Rep. NRS-GTR-276. Newtown Square, PA: U.S. Department of Agriculture, Forest Service, Northern Research Station: 11–19.

Emery, M.R.; Ginger, C.; Newman, S.; Giammusso, M.R.B. 2003. Special forest products in context: gatherers and gathering in the Eastern United States. Gen. Tech. Rep. NRS-GTR-306. Newtown Square, PA: U.S. Department of Agriculture, Forest Service, Northern Research Station. 59 p.

Emery, M.R.; Pierce, A.R. 2005. Interrupting the telos: locating subsistence in contemporary U.S. forests. Environment and Planning. A37(6): 981–993.

Flather, C.H.; Brady, S.J.; Knowles, M.S. 1999. Wildlife resource trends in the United States: a technical document supporting the 2000 USDA Forest Service RPA assessment. Gen. Tech. Rep. RMRS-GTR-33. Fort Collins, CO: U.S. Department of Agriculture, Forest Service, Rocky Mountain Research Station. 79 p.

Flather, C.H.; Michael, S.K.; Brady, S.J. 2009. Population and harvest trends of big game and small game species: a technical document supporting the USDA Forest Service interim update of the 2000 RPA assessment. RMRS-GTR-219. Fort Collins, CO: U.S. Department of Agriculture, Forest Service, Rocky Mountain Research Station. 34 p.

Forest and Rangeland Renewable Resources Planning Act of 1974; 16 U.S.C. 1601 (note).

Forsyth, D.J.; Gramling, R.; Wooddell, G. 1998. The game of poaching: folk crimes in Southwest Louisiana. Society and Natural Resources. 11: 25–28.

Hufford, M. 2000. Tending the commons: folklife and landscape in southern West Virginia. Washington, DC: American Folklife Center, Library of Congress. http://memory.loc.gov/ammem/collections/tending. (August 3, 2010).

Jones, E.T.; Lynch, K.A. 2007. Nontimber forest products and biodiversity management in the Pacific Northwest. Forest Ecology and Management. 246: 29–37.

Love, T.; Jones, E.; Liegel, L. 1998. Valuing the temperate rainforest: wild mushrooming on the Olympic Peninsula Biosphere Reserve. Ambio Special Report. 9: 16–25.

Morrison, H.S.I.; Marsinko, A.; Guynn, D. 2002. Selected characteristics of forest industry hunt-lease programs in the South. In: Smathers, W.M., Jr.; Bergstrom, J.C., eds. Issues in wildlife economies and the ecology-economy interface. Southern Natural Resources Economics-Information Exchange Group. SERA-IEG-30 workshop proceedings. Mississippi State, MS: Southern Rural Development Center: 27–34.

Muir, P.S. 2004. An assessment of commercial "moss" harvesting from forested lands in the Pacific Northwestern and Appalachian Regions of the United States: How much moss is harvested and sold domestically and internationally and which species are involved? Final report to U.S. Fish and Wildlife Service and U.S. Geological Survey, Forest and Rangeland Ecosystem Science Center. Oregon State University, Oregon. http://oregonstate.edu/~mccuneb/MuirReport. htm. (May 13, 2009).

Muir, P.S.; Norman, K.N.; Sikes, K.G. 2006. Quantity and value of commercial moss harvest from forests of the Pacific Northwest and Appalachian regions of the U.S. The Bryologist. 109(2): 197–214.

National Christmas Tree Association [NCTA]. 2009. Quick tree facts. http://www.christmastree.org/facts.cfm. (May 13, 2009).

Peck, J.E. 2006. Towards sustainable commercial moss harvest in the Pacific Northwest of North America. Biological Conservation. 28(3): 289–297.

Peck, J.E.; Muir, P.S. 2007. Are they harvesting what we think they're harvesting? Comparing field data to commercially sold forest moss. Biodiversity and Conservation. 16(7): 2031–2043.

Peck, J.E.; Muir, P.S. 2008. Biomass inventory and regrowth rate of harvestable epiphytic moss in the Oregon Coast Range. Western Journal of Applied Forestry. 23(1): 34–39.

Peña, D.G. 1999. Cultural landscapes and biodiversity: the ethnoecology of an upper Río Grande watershed commons. In: Nazarea, V.D., ed. Ethnoecology: situated knowledge/located lives. Tucson, AZ: University of Arizona Press: 107–132.

Pilz, D.; Alexander, S.J.; Smith, J.; Schroeder, R.; Freed, J. 2006. Nontimber forest product opportunities in Alaska. Gen. Tech. Rep. PNW-GTR-671. Portland, OR: U.S. Department of Agriculture, Forest Service, Pacific Northwest Research Station. 79 p.

Pilz, D.; Molina, R. 2002. Commercial harvests of edible mushrooms from the forests of the Pacific Northwest United States: issues, management, and monitoring for sustainability. Forest Ecology and Management. 155(1-3): 3–16.

Raish, C. 2000. Environmentalism, the Forest Service, and the Hispano communities of northern New Mexico. Society and Natural Resources. 13: 489–508.

Schroeder, R. 2002. Contemporary subsistence use of nontimber forest products in Alaska. In: Jones, E.T.; McLain, R.J.; Weigand, J., eds. Nontimber forest products of the United States. Lawrence, KS: University Press of Kansas: 300–326.

Smith, J.; Crone, L.K.; Alexander, S.J. 2010. A U.S. Forest Service special forest products appraisal system: background, methods, and assessment. Gen. Tech. Rep. PNW-GTR-822. Portland, OR: U.S. Department of Agriculture, Forest Service, Pacific Northwest Research Station. 22 p.

U.S. Department of Agriculture, Forest Service [USDA FS]. 2004. National report on sustainable forests—2003. FS-766, Washington, DC: U.S. Department of Agriculture, Forest Service. 139 p.

U.S. Department of Agriculture, Forest Service [USDA FS]. 2007. Automated timber sale accounting: nontimber contract and permit data, 1998–2007. [Database].

U.S. Department of Agriculture, National Agricultural Statistics Service [USDA NASS]. 2007. Maple syrup 2007: June 12. New England Agricultural statistics bulletin. http://www.agmrc.org. (May 13, 2009).

U.S. Department of the Interior, Bureau of Land Management. [USDI BLM]. 2007. Automated timber sale information system: nontimber contract and permit data, 1998–2007. [Database].

U.S. Department of the Interior, Fish and Wildlife Service [USDI]; U.S. Department of Commerce, Census Bureau [USDOC]. 2006. National survey of fishing, hunting, and wildlife-associated recreation. [Place of publication unknown]. 164 p.

U.S. International Trade Commission. 2008. U.S. imports/exports data (Dataweb). http://www.usitc.gov/. (May 13, 2009).

Wolfe, R.J. 2000. Subsistence in Alaska: a year 2000 update. Juneau, AK: Division of Subsistence, Alaska Department of Fish and Game. 4 p.

Wolfe, R.J. 2001. Subsistence food production and distribution in Alaska: social organization, management, and development issues. INUSSUK, Arctic Research Journal. 1: 213–231.

World Commission on Environment and Development [WCED]. 1987. Our common future. Oxford, United Kingdom: Oxford University Press. 400 p.